# A Gift of Encouragement

*for*

_____

*from*

_____

# Encouragement

JOHN C. MAXWELL

*Bless and be Blessed*

# CHANGES
# EVERYTHING

THOMAS NELSON
*Since 1798*

NASHVILLE   DALLAS   MEXICO CITY   RIO DE JANEIRO   BEIJING

Published in Nashville, TN, by Thomas Nelson. Thomas Nelson
is a trademark of Thomas Nelson, Inc.

Thomas Nelson, Inc., titles may be purchased in bulk for educational,
business, fundraising, or sales promotional use. For information,
please email SpecialMarkets@ThomasNelson.com.

Unless otherwise indicated, all scripture references are from *The New
King James Version of the Bible* (NKJV) ©1979, 1980, 1982, 1992,
Thomas Nelson, Inc., Publisher. All rights reserved. *The Holy Bible,
New Living Translation* (NLT) © 1996. Used by permission of Tyndale
House Publishers, Inc., Wheaton, Ill. All rights reserved. *The New
International Version of the Bible* (NIV) © 1984 by the International
Bible Society. Used by permission of Zondervan Bible Publishers. All
rights reserved.

Designed by Lookout Design, Inc. | Minneapolis, Minnesota

ISBN–10: 1-4041-0423-2
ISBN–13: 978-1-4041-0423-5

Printed and bound in China

www.thomasnelson.com

*Encouragement is*

*oxygen to the soul.*

GEORGE MATTHEW ADAMS

# INTRODUCTION
*Encourage Others and Change Their Worlds*

Everyone needs encouragement. And everyone—young or old, the successful or less-than-successful, unknown or famous—who receives encouragement is changed by it. As Mark Twain said, "One compliment can keep me going for a whole month."

Encouragement's impact can be profound. A word of encouragement from a teacher to a child can change his life. A word of encouragement from a spouse can save a marriage. A word of encouragement from a leader can inspire a person to reach her potential. Like Zig Ziglar says, "You never know when a moment and a few sincere words can have an impact on a life."

What does true encouragement look like—the kind that changes lives forever? To encourage people is to help them gain courage they might not otherwise possess—courage to face the day, to do what's right, to take risks, to make a difference. And the heart of encouragement is to communicate a person's value. When we help people feel valuable, capable, and motivated we sometimes see their lives change forever—and then see them go on to change the world.

If you are a parent, you have a responsibility to encourage members of your family. If you are an organizational leader, the effectiveness of your team increases dramatically in proportion to the amount of encouragement you give the people you lead. As a friend, you have the privilege of sharing encouraging words that may help someone persevere through a rough time or strive for greatness. In the following pages, we'll see how encouragement has the power to change everything—individuals, families, schools, businesses, churches—by creating an environment where people can become their best.

I hope this book is an encouragement to you. I trust the stories, quotes, and observations will help and inspire you. And once you have been encouraged, I pray you will pass that encouragement on to others. Never forget: Encouragement changes everything. Bless and be blessed!

God's love *for* us gives us
the *reason* to encourage others.

God's love *in* us gives us
the *ability* to encourage others.

God's love *through* us gives us
the *way* to encourage others.

John C. Maxwell

Be of good courage,

and He shall strengthen your heart,

all you who hope in the LORD.

PSALM 31:24

# *Encouragement*

# Keeps Us Going

*People go farther than they thought they could
when someone else thinks they can.*

JOHN C. MAXWELL

*Let no feeling of discouragement*

*prey upon you, and in the end*

*you are sure to succeed.*

Abraham Lincoln

# A WORD TO THE WISE

Nineteenth-century writer Walt Whitman struggled for years to get anyone interested in his poetry. In the midst of his discouragement, Whitman received a life-changing letter from an admirer of his work. The note read: "Dear sir, I am not blind to the worth of the wonderful gift of *Leaves of Grass*. I find it the most extraordinary piece of wit and wisdom that America has yet contributed. I greet you at the beginning of a great career." It was signed by Ralph Waldo Emerson.

Whitman enjoyed a long career and is now considered one of the giants of American literature. But when times were tough, he needed encouragement to keep going. When we're on the brink of failure, the right words at the right time can keep us in the game. When we're too tired or discouraged to keep going, an act of compassion can give us new strength. There's no doubt about it: Encouragement enables us to persevere like nothing else.

# ENCOURAGEMENT AND ENDURANCE

When Rick Hoyt was born in 1962, his parents possessed the typical excited expectations of first-time parents. But then they discovered that during Rick's birth, his umbilical cord had been wrapped around his neck, cutting off the oxygen to his brain. Later, Rick was diagnosed with cerebral palsy. "When he was eight months old," his father, Dick, remembers, "the doctors told us we should put him away—he'd be a vegetable all his life."[1] But Rick's parents wouldn't do that. They were determined to raise him like any other child.

AN UPHILL BATTLE. Sometimes that was tough. Rick is a quadriplegic who cannot speak because he has limited control of his tongue. But Rick's parents worked with him, encouraged him, and taught him everything they could, always including him in family activities. When Rick was ten, his life changed when engineers from Tufts University created a device that enabled him to communicate via computer. The first words he slowly and painstakingly punched out were, "Go Bruins." That's when the family, who had been following the NHL's Boston Bruins in the playoffs, discovered Rick was a sports fan.

One day in school when he was fifteen, Rick found out about a fundraising 5K race (3.1 miles) intended to help a young athlete who had been paralyzed in an accident. He told his father that he wanted to participate. Dick, a lieutenant colonel in the Air National Guard (now retired), was in his late thirties and out of shape. But he wanted to encourage his son, so he agreed to run and push his son in a modified wheelchair. When they crossed the finish line (second to last), Dick recalls, Rick flashed "the biggest smile you ever saw in your life." After the race, Rick wrote out this simple message: "Dad, I felt like I wasn't handicapped." After that day, their lives would never be the same again.

WORKING TOGETHER. What does a father do when his son, who has never been out of a wheelchair, says that he loves to race? He becomes his boy's hands and feet. That's the day "Team Hoyt" was born. Dick bought Rick a more sophisticated racing chair. Then the quadriplegic teenager and the out-of-shape dad began running together—and not just casually. Before long, they began training seriously, and in 1984, they ran in their first Boston Marathon together. After that they hadn't missed a Boston Marathon in twenty years.

After four years of running marathons, the two decided that they were ready for another challenge: triathlons, which combine swimming, cycling, and running. That was no small challenge, especially since Dick would have to learn how to swim! But he did. Dick explained, "Rick's the one who has motivated me because if it wasn't for him, I wouldn't be out there competing. What I'm doing is loaning Rick my arms and legs so he can be out there competing like everybody else."[2]

Of all the triathlon races in the world, one is considered the toughest—the Ironman in Hawaii. The race consists of three back-to-back legs: a 2.4 mile swim, a 112 mile bike race, and a full marathon run of 26.2 miles. It's an excruciating test of stamina for any individual. In 1989, Dick and Rick competed in the race together. For the swimming portion, Dick towed a small boat with Rick in it. Then he biked for the 112 miles with Rick in a seat on his bicycle's handlebars. By the time they got to the running portion, Dick was exhausted.

But Dick wasn't going to let Rick down. All he had to do was think of the encouragement his son received when they competed. Rick's words must have rung in his ears:

"When I'm running, my disability seems to disappear. It is the only place where truly I feel as an equal. Due to all the positive feedback, I do not feel handicapped at all. Rather, I feel that I am the intelligent person that I am with no limits."[3]

Lifting up his son was what made all the training and pain worthwhile. Dick loaded Rick into his running chair, and off they went to finish the Ironman. The two of them finished the race in a little over 13 hours and 43 minutes—a very strong time.

Since then, Rick has earned his college degree, and he works at Boston University helping to design computer systems for people with disabilities. And of course, he still competes with his father, who is now over 65 years old. By competing, they encourage each other. As of March 2007, Team Hoyt has completed a total of

942 races. They've run 65 marathons and 246 triathlons, including six races at Ironman distances. And they will keep running. "There is nothing in the world that the both of us can't conquer together," says Dick.[4] That is the power of encouragement.

ADAPTED FROM

*The 17 Indisputable Laws of Teamwork*

There are three kinds of people in the world today. There are *"well-poisoners,"* who discourage you and stomp on your creativity and tell you what you can't do. There are *"lawn-mowers,"* people who are well-intentioned but self-absorbed; they tend to their own needs, mow their own lawns, and never leave their yards to help another person. Finally, there are *"life-enhancers,"* people who reach out to enrich the lives of others, to lift them up and inspire them. We need to be life-enhancers, and we need to surround ourselves with life-enhancers.

WALT DISNEY

*When someone does*

*something good,*

*applaud!*

*You will make*

*two people happy.*

SAMUEL GOLDWYN

# ENCOURAGING THE ENCOURAGER

One day recently when my wife, Margaret, answered the phone, she talked for a moment, then looked at me with her hand over the mouthpiece and asked, "Do you know a Dick Vermeil?"

I practically knocked her down trying to get to the phone.

Vermeil is a coaching legend. He started as a high school coach in 1959 and coached football at every level. He's been named Coach of the Year on four levels: high school, junior college, NCAA Division I, and the NFL. In the 1990s, he came out of retirement to coach the St. Louis Rams, and in 1999, he won the Super Bowl with them. Was it really Dick Vermeil? And why in the world would he be calling me?

It turns out it really was Dick Vermeil. He was calling me because of something I had taught for Maximum Impact, the CD lesson that more than fifteen thousand subscribers receive from me every month. I had mentioned that when I read an excellent book and I take away a lot from it, I jot a note to the author to say thank you and let him or her know what the work meant to me. All teachers want to hear that their work is making a difference.

Vermeil was calling to let me know that he's been reading my books and receiving my CDs for six years. He's listened to the lessons in his car to and from practice, and he sometimes shares the principles with his coaches and players. He just wanted to let me know.

It was a real privilege to chat with him. That kind of encouragement can energize a person for a long time!

Take some time to contact someone who has encouraged you. Let the person know what his or her work has meant to you. Everybody needs encouragement!

*The way you see people is the way you treat them.*
*And the way you treat them is the way they often become.*

JOHN C. MAXWELL

I played football in college. I wasn't
very big—only 150 pounds—and I wasn't very
good. I got hurt a lot. I broke my arm once,
my neck once, and my nose six times.
When I tell people about it, they always ask me,
"Why did you keep doing it?" For the longest
time I had no answer. Then one day it hit me.
If there hadn't been any fans in the stands
cheering me on—my family and friends—I
wouldn't have kept on playing and trying so
hard. But there were, so I did.

TOM MALONE,
*former President and COO of Milliken and Company*

*Faith makes*

*all things possible.*

*Love makes*

*all things worthwhile.*

# An Experiment in Encouragement

Years ago an experiment was
conducted to measure people's
capacity to endure pain. How long
could a bare-footed person stand in
a bucket of ice water? It was
discovered that when there was
someone else present offering
encouragement and support, the
person standing in the ice water
could tolerate pain twice as long as
when no one else was present.

*Encouragement is deciding*

*to make your problem my problem.*

JOHN C. MAXWELL

## GREAT TALENT NEEDS ENCOURAGEMENT

George Frederick Handel was a musical prodigy. Though his father wanted him to study law, he gravitated to music at an early age. By age seventeen, he held the post of church organist at the Cathedral in Halle, his hometown. A year later, he became a violinist and harpsichordist at the Kaiser's Opera House in Hamburg. By age twenty-one, he was a keyboard virtuoso. When he turned to composing, he gained immediate fame and soon was appointed Kapellmeister to the elector of Hanover (later King George I of England). When Handel moved to England, his renown grew. By the time he was forty, he was world famous.

But despite Handel's talent and fame, he faced considerable adversity. Competition with rival English composers was fierce. Audiences were fickle and sometimes didn't turn out for his performances. He was frequently the victim of the changing political winds. Several times he found himself penniless and on the verge of bankruptcy. The pain of rejection and failure was difficult, especially following his previous success.

Then his problems were compounded by failing health. He suffered a kind of seizure or stroke, which left his right arm limp and damaged the use of four fingers on his right hand. Although he recovered, it left him despondent.

Finally, in 1741, Handel decided it was time to retire even though he was only fifty-six. He was discouraged, miserable, and consumed with debt. He felt certain he would land in debtor's prison. So on April 8, he gave what he considered his farewell concert. Disappointed and filled with self-pity, he gave up.

But in August of that year, something incredible happened. A wealthy friend named Charles Jennings encouraged Handel by visiting him and giving him a libretto based on the life of Christ. The work intrigued Handel enough to stir him to action. He began writing. Immediately the floodgates of inspiration opened in him. For three weeks, he wrote almost nonstop. Then he spent another two days creating the orchestrations. In twenty-four days, he had completed the 260-page manuscript of *Messiah*.

Today, *Handel's Messiah* is considered a masterpiece and the culmination of the composer's work. In fact, Sir Newman Flower, one of the Handel's biographers, said of the writing of *Messiah*, "Considering the immensity of the work, and the short time involved, it will remain, perhaps forever, the greatest feat in the whole history of music composition."

FROM *Failing Forward*

# Encourage Yourself

Don't let yourself . . .

Worry when you're doing your best.

Hurry when success depends on accuracy.

Think evil of anyone until you have the facts.

Believe a thing is impossible without trying it.

Waste time on trivial matters.

Imagine that good intentions are a
satisfactory excuse.

Harbor bitterness toward God or person.

He who has begun a good work

in you will complete it

until the day of Jesus Christ.

PHILIPPIANS 4:6

*Encouragement*

# Makes Us Better

There are high spots in all of our lives
and most of them have come about
through encouragement from someone else.

GEORGE M. ADAMS

*Treat a man
as he appears to be
and you make him worse.
But treat a man
as if he already were
what he potentially could be,
and you make him
what he should be.*

GOETHE

## BELIEVE IN YOURSELF

Several years ago, an experiment was performed in a school in the San Francisco Bay area. A principal called in three teachers and said, "Because you three teachers are the finest in the system and you have the greatest expertise, we're going to give you ninety selected high-IQ students. We're going to let you move these students through this next year at their pace and see how much they can learn."

The three faculty members, the students, and the students' parents thought this was a great idea. And it seemed they especially enjoyed the school year. By the time school was through, the students had achieved from 20 to 30 percent more than the other students in the entire San Francisco Bay area.

At the end of the year, the principal called the three teachers in and told them, "I have a confession to make. You did not have ninety of the most intellectually prominent students. They were run-of-the-mill students. We took ninety students at random from the system and gave them to you."

The teachers naturally concluded that their exceptional teaching skills must have been responsible for the students' great progress.

"I have another confession," said the principal. "You're not the brightest of the teachers. Your names were the first three drawn out of a hat."[5]

Why, then, did those students and teachers perform at such an exceptional level for an entire year? They were encouraged to believe they could!

ADAPTED FROM *Your Roadmap to Success*

*I'll tell you what makes a great manager:*

*a great manager has a knack for making ballplayers*

*think they are better than they are.*

*He forces you to have a good opinion of yourself.*

*He lets you know he believes in you.*

*He makes you get more out of yourself.*

*And once you learn how good you really are,*

*you never settle for playing anything less*

*than your very best.*

REGGIE JACKSON

*I have yet to find the man,*

*however exalted his station,*

*who did not do better work*

*and put forth greater effort*

*under a spirit of approval*

*than under a spirit of criticism.*

CHARLES SCHWAB

# *Positively Wired*

A study was done by psychologist Henry H. Goddard on energy levels in children. He hooked children up to a device called an ergograph to see how they would respond to the words of others. He found that when tired children were given a word of praise or commendation, the ergograph showed they experienced an immediate surge in energy. But when the children were criticized or discouraged, the device showed their energy took a sudden nosedive.

Never underestimate the power of an encouraging word.

*Speak up TODAY and say something positive.*

*Even a tombstone will say something*

*good about people when they are dead.*

JOHN C. MAXWELL

# EVERYONE APPRECIATES
# A KIND WORD

In the 1920s, physician, consultant, and psychologist George W. Crane began teaching social psychology at Northwestern University in Chicago. Though he was new to teaching, he was an astute student of human nature, and he believed strongly in making the study of psychology practical to his students.

One of the first classes he taught contained evening students who were older than the average college student. The young men and women worked in the department stores, offices, and factories of Chicago by day and were trying to improve themselves by attending classes at night.

After class one evening a young woman named Lois, who had moved to Chicago from a small town in Wisconsin to take a civil service job, confided in Crane that she felt isolated and lonely.

"I don't know anybody except a few girls at the office," she lamented. "At night I go to my room and write letters home. The only thing that keeps me living from day to day is the hope of receiving a letter from my friends in Wisconsin."

It was largely in response to Lois's problem that Crane came up with what he called the Compliment Club, which he announced to his class the following week. It was to be the first of several practical assignments he would give them that term.

"You are to use your psychology every day either at home or at work or on the streetcars and buses," Crane told them. "For the first month, your written assignment will be the *Compliment Club*. Every day you are to pay an honest compliment to each of three different persons. You can increase that number if you wish, but to qualify for a class grade, you must have complimented at least three people every day for thirty days. . . . Then, at the end of the thirty-day experiment, I want you to write a theme or paper on your experiences," he continued. "Include the changes you have noted in the people around you, as well as your own altered outlook on life."[6]

Some of Crane's students resisted this assignment. Some complained that they wouldn't know what to say. Others were afraid of being rejected. And a few thought it would be dishonest to compliment someone they didn't like. "Suppose you meet somebody you dislike?" one man asked. "Wouldn't it be insincere to praise your enemy?"

"No, it is not insincerity when you compliment your enemy," Crane responded, "for the compliment is an honest statement of praise for some objective trait or merit that deserves commendation. You will find that nobody is entirely devoid of merit or virtue. . . . Your praise may buoy up the morale of lonely souls who are almost ready to give up the struggle to do good deeds. You never know when your casual compliment may catch a boy or girl, or man or woman, at the critical point when he would otherwise toss in the sponge."[7]

Crane's students discovered that their sincere compliments had a positive impact on the people around them, and the experience made an even greater impact on the students themselves. Lois blossomed into a real people person who lit up a room when she entered it. Another student, who was ready to quit her job as a legal secretary because of an especially difficult boss, began complimenting him, even though at first she did so through clenched teeth. Eventually not only did his surliness toward her change, but so did her exasperation with him. They wound up taking a genuine liking to each other and were married.

George Crane's Compliment Club probably sounds a little bit corny to us today. But the principles behind it are just as sound now as they were in the 1920s. The bottom line is that Crane was teaching what I call the Elevator Principle: We can lift people up or take people down in our relationships. He was trying to teach his students to be proactive. Crane said, "The world is starving for appreciation. It is hungry for compliments. But somebody must start the ball rolling by speaking first and saying a nice thing to his companion."[8] He embraced the sentiment of Benjamin Franklin, who believed, "As we must account for every idle word—so we must for every idle silence."

FROM *Winning with People*

*You will find as you look*

*back upon your life*

*that the moments when*

*you have really lived,*

*are the moments when*

*you have done things*

*in a spirit of love.*

HENRY DRUMMOND

*The greatest good you can do*

*for another is not*

*just share your riches,*

*but to reveal to him his own.*

BENJAMIN DISRAELI

# Help People Get
## What They Want

Psychologists say that deep down, all people have certain desires in common. If you want to encourage people, help them fulfill these most basic, heartfelt desires:

People want to do the right thing—stand with them.

People want to find better ways of doing things—empower them.

People want to achieve things of which they can be proud—motivate them.

People want to belong to a group that achieves the extraordinary—invite them.

People want to earn recognition for who they are and what they achieve—honor them.

*How do you identify someone*

*who needs encouragement?*

*That person is breathing.*

TRUETT CATHEY

# TAKE OTHERS TO A HIGHER LEVEL

I believe that deep down everyone wants to become an encourager—even the most negative person. We all want to be a positive influence in the lives of others. And we can be. If you want to lift people up and add value to their lives, keep the following in mind.

ENCOURAGERS COMMIT THEMSELVES TO GIVING OTHERS ENCOURAGEMENT DAILY. Roman philosopher Lucius Annaeus Seneca observed, "Wherever there is a human being, there is an opportunity for kindness." If you want to lift people up, do it daily.

ENCOURAGERS KNOW THE LITTLE DIFFERENCE THAT SEPARATES HURTING AND HELPING. The little things you do every day have a greater impact on others than you might think. You hold the power to make another person's life better or worse by the things you do today. Those closest to you—your spouse, children, or parents—are most affected by what you say and do. Use that power wisely.

ENCOURAGERS INITIATE THE POSITIVE IN A NEGATIVE ENVIRONMENT. It's one thing to be positive in a positive or neutral environment. It's another to be an instrument of change in a negative environment. Yet that's what encouragers try to do. Sometimes that requires a kind word, other times it takes a servant's action, and occasionally it calls for creativity.

ENCOURAGERS UNDERSTAND LIFE IS NOT A DRESS REHEARSAL. Here's a quote I've always loved: "I expect to pass through this world but once. Any good therefore that I can do, or any kindness that I can show to any fellow creature, let me do it now. Let me not defer or neglect it, for I shall not pass this way again." People who lift others don't wait until tomorrow or some other "better" day to help people. They act now!

Everyone can become an encourager. You don't have to be rich. You don't have to be a genius. You don't have to have it all together. All you have to do is care about people and initiate.

ADAPTED FROM *Winning with People*

# It Takes Just a Little

It takes so little to make us sad,

Just a slighting word or a doubting sneer,

Just a scornful smile on some lips held dear;

And our footsteps lag, though the goal seemed near,

And we lose the courage and hope we had—

So little it takes to make us sad.

It takes so little to make us glad,

Just a cheering clasp of a friendly hand,

Just a word from one who can understand;

And we finish the task we long had planned,

And we lose the doubt and the fear we had—

So little it takes to make us glad.

IDA GOLDSMITH MORRIS

*Flatter me,*

*and I may not believe you.*

*Criticize me,*

*and I may not like you.*

*Ignore me,*

*and I may not forgive you.*

*Encourage me,*

*and I will not forget you.*

WILLIAM ARTHUR WARD

*Life is a great obstacle course,*

*with bends and turns, wins and losses.*

*When you get to the high jump,*

*always remember to throw your heart*

*over the bar—and the rest will follow.*

MICHELE LEONARD

Let Your mercy, O LORD, be upon us,

Just as we hope in You.

PSALM 33:22

# Encouragement

# Gives Us Hope

Faith keeps the person that keeps the faith.

MOTHER TERESA

*The secret of encouragement is hope.*

JOHN C. MAXWELL

## KEEPING HOPE ALIVE

When Sir Ernest Shackleton set out to sea in 1914, he did so with the ambitious goal of making the first land crossing of Antarctica. But his ship, the *Endurance*, never even reached its base camp. It became stuck in the icy waters for months and eventually sank. Shackleton and his twenty-seven-member crew were stranded more than twelve hundred miles from civilization, drifting on ice floes in the terrifying cold with just three rickety lifeboats, a few tents, and limited provisions.

Eventually, they reached a small island and waited while Shackleton and a handful of men took one of the lifeboats eight hundred miles over tumultuous seas to a whaling station. Shackleton returned with a rescue ship, and every man survived the eighteen-month ordeal.

How did he keep the hopes of his men from fizzling out? First, he modeled optimism. Shackleton, who once described optimism as "true moral courage," always believed he and his crew would survive, and his optimism was contagious. He communicated that optimism to everyone around him.

Second, he nurtured his men's sense of significance. He kept everyone involved by seeking their opinions and by giving them tasks that made them feel like they were part of the solution.

He also encouraged them with humor and promoted a lighthearted atmosphere. Shackleton recognized that under extreme pressure, the ability to lighten the mood neutralizes fear and enables a team to focus, reenergize, and prevail over daunting obstacles. People might find it strange that one of the few items that Shackleton rescued from the sinking ship was a crewman's banjo. He did it so the group could have music.

It was Napoleon who said that a leader is a dealer in hope, and Shackleton was a prime example of how one person can keep hope alive.

If you know someone who is in the middle of a difficult trial—a long illness or a period of financial strain—your words of kindness and love, your confidence in them, your ability to lighten their load can bring hope and encouragement to their lives.

# How to Fight Discouragement

Reject rejection.

See mistakes as temporary.

See failures as isolated incidents.

Keep expectations positive.

Focus on strengths.

Vary your approach to achievement.

Bounce back.

There are none in the humanly "down"

position so low that they cannot be lifted up

by entering God's order, and none in the

humanly "up" position so high that they

can disregard God's point of view on their

lives. The barren, the widow, the orphan,

the eunuch, the alien, all models of human

hopelessness, are fruitful and secure in

God's care.

DALLAS WILLARD,
*The Divine Conspiracy*

# Encouraging a President

An exhibit at the Smithsonian Institution displays the personal effects carried by President Abraham Lincoln on the night he was shot: a small handkerchief embroidered "A. Lincoln," a pen knife of the type carried by a country boy, a spectacle case with cotton string, a Confederate five-dollar bill, and a worn-out newspaper clipping extolling his accomplishments as president, that starts out, "Abe Lincoln is one of the greatest statesmen of all time...."

Why would Lincoln—considered by many to be the Unites States' greatest president—carry such an article? Because Lincoln led during one of the country's most difficult times. He was often criticized, vilified, and threatened. Sometimes he needed to be reminded that somebody believed in him.

*He will shield you*

*with his wings.*

*He will shelter you*

*with his feathers.*

*His faithful promises*

*are your armor*

*and protection.*

PSALM 91:4 NLT

# Hope in the Lord

Psalm 91 is one of the most comforting passages in the Bible. It describes the security believers can enjoy through faith in God, and its promises paint a profound portrait of hope. Reflect on this hope—breathe it in deep—then go out and share it with others.

| GOD'S PROMISE | YOUR BENEFIT |
| --- | --- |
| His presence | *You don't have to be lonely, no matter what you're going through.* |
| His protection | *As you take initiative and risks, God keeps you safe.* |
| His peace | *You don't have to feel insecure in unknown territory* |
| His perspective | *God gives an eternal view of life that keeps you steady.* |
| His provision | *Regardless of your needs, God meets them.* |
| His power | *In adversity, God delivers and helps you reach your goal.* |

*Sometimes our light goes out*

*but is blown into flame by another human being.*

*Each of us owes deepest thanks*

*to those who have rekindled this light.*

ALBERT SCHWEITZER

# DO THE MATH

There are really four kinds of people when it comes to relationships.

1. SOME PEOPLE ADD SOMETHING TO LIFE—*we enjoy them*. Many people in this world desire to help others. These people are adders. They make the lives of others more pleasant and enjoyable. Evangelist John Wesley advised people to . . .

> *do all the good you can,*
> *by all the means you can,*
> *in all the ways you can,*
> *in all the places you can,*
> *at all the times you can,*
> *to all the people you can,*
> *as long as ever you can.*

Wesley was an adder.

People who add value to others almost always do so *intentionally*. I say that because adding value to others requires a person to give of himself, and that rarely occurs by accident. I have endeavored to become an adder. I like people and I want to help them. I make it my goal to be a friend.

Recently the CEO of a large corporation invited me to speak on leadership for his organization. After teaching his executives and conducting sessions for his managers, I had gained enough credibility with him that he wanted to do something nice for me.

"John, I like what you've done for us," he said as we sat one day in his office. "Now, what can I do for you?"

"Nothing," I replied. "You don't need to do anything for me." The corporation had, of course, paid me for the times I had spoken, and I had really enjoyed the experience. His people were sharp and eager to learn.

"Oh, come on," he said. "Everybody wants *something*. What do you want?"

"Look, doesn't everybody need an easy friend? Somebody who doesn't want anything?" I answered, looking him in the eye. "I just want to be an easy friend."

He chuckled and said, "Okay, you'll be my easy friend." And that's who I have endeavored to be. Author Frank Tyger says, "Friendship consists of a willing ear, an understanding heart, and a helping hand." That's what I'm trying to give my friend.

2. SOME PEOPLE SUBTRACT SOMETHING FROM LIFE— *we tolerate them.* In *Julius Caesar,* Cassius asserts, "A friend should bear his friend's infirmities, / But Brutus makes mine greater than they are." That's what subtracters do. They do not bear our burdens, and they make heavier the ones we already have. The sad thing about subtracters is that what they

do is usually unintentional. If you don't know how to add to others, then you probably subtract by default.

In relationships, receiving is easy. Giving is much more difficult. It's similar to the difference between building something and tearing it down. It takes a skilled craftsman much time and energy to build a beautiful chair. It takes no skill whatsoever to smash that chair in a matter of moments.

3. SOME PEOPLE MULTIPLY SOMETHING IN LIFE— *we value them.* Anyone who wants to can become an adder. It takes only a desire to lift people up and the intentionality to follow through. That is what George Crane was trying to teach his students when he instituted the Compliment Club. But to go to another level in relationships—to become a multiplier— one must be intentional, strategic, and skilled. The greater the talent and resources a person possesses, the greater his potential to become a multiplier.

I am fortunate. I have a lot of multipliers in my life, highly gifted people who want to see me succeed, people such as John Hull, David Hoyt, and Tom Mullins. These men have servants' hearts. They are tops in their fields. They value partnership. They're always generating great ideas. And they're passionate about making a difference. They help me sharpen my vision and maximize my strengths.

You probably have people like that in your life, people who live to help you succeed and have the skills to help you along the way. If you can think of people who have played the role of multiplier in your life, stop and take some time to call or write them and let them know what they've meant in your life.

4. SOME PEOPLE DIVIDE SOMETHING IN LIFE— *we avoid them.* R. G. LeTourneau, who founded Caterpillar, a manufacturer of large earthmoving equipment, says his company used to make a scraper that was known as Model G. One day a customer asked a salesman what the *G* stood for. The salesman, like many people in his profession, was quick on his feet, and he replied, "The *G* stands for gossip because like a talebearer, this machine moves a lot of dirt and moves it fast!"

Dividers are people who will really "take you to the basement," meaning they'll take you down as low as they can, as often as they can. They're like the company president who sent his personnel director a memo, saying, "Search the organization for an alert, aggressive young man who could step into my shoes—and when you find him, fire him."

Dividers are so damaging because unlike subtracters, their negative actions are usually intentional. They are hurtful people who make themselves look or feel better by trying to make someone else do worse than they do. As a result, they damage relationships and create havoc in people's lives.

FROM *Winning with People*

# The Six Most Encouraging Phrases

I love you.

Dinner is served.

All is forgiven.

Keep the change.

You've lost weight.

I believe in you.

*Behold, I will do a new thing,*

*Now it shall spring forth;*

*Shall you not know it?*

*I will even make a road in the wilderness*

*And rivers in the desert.*

Isaiah 43:19

Encouragement

# Turns Lives Around

There are people who think seeing obstacles

is a sign of maturity and insight.

But anyone of average intelligence can do that.

God wants people who see a way beyond the obstacles

and who encourage others to take it.

*People want to be appreciated,*

*not impressed.*

*They want to be regarded*

*as human beings,*

*not as sounding boards*

*for other people's egos.*

*They want to be treated*

*as an end in themselves,*

*not as a means toward*

*the gratification of*

*another's vanity.*

SYDNEY J. HARRIS

# 5 THINGS EVERY ENCOURAGER NEEDS TO KNOW ABOUT PEOPLE

You have tremendous power to affect the lives of people around you. Encouragement from you could be the difference-maker in someone's day, week, or even life, sending that person in a whole new direction.

It's difficult to encourage people if you don't know what encourages them. Become a student of people. Learn what makes them tick. Know what lifts them up.

To get you started, begin by embracing these five things I know about people:

## 1. EVERYBODY WANTS TO BE SOMEBODY.

Every person wants to be affirmed. Every person wants to be loved. Every person wants to be well considered. Everybody wants to be somebody. That is true from the smallest of children to the oldest adults.

How can you help other people to feel like they are somebody? By seeing them as a ten. I believe that you get out of people exactly what you expect from them. If you treat people like tens, they respond like tens. If you treat someone like two, he responds like a two. People want recognition and affirmation. It is a deep human desire, and we can help people become great simply by showing them how we believe in them.

## 2. NOBODY CARES HOW MUCH YOU KNOW UNTIL THEY KNOW HOW MUCH YOU CARE.

People don't want to know how smart we are. They don't want to know what you or I have accomplished. The only thing they really want to know from us, first of all, is whether we really care about them.

This is a difficult lesson for some leaders to learn. They want to impress people. They want others to admire them. They want others to follow them. Most followers don't care about all that. True, they want leaders who display competence and character. But most of all, followers want to know that their leaders care about them and have their interests at heart.

## 3. EVERYBODY NEEDS SOMEBODY.

In the movie *Remember the Titans*, the true story of Coach Herman Boone as he led a newly racially integrated football team to victory, Coach Boone stands talking to Louie Lastik, a bighearted offensive lineman. When he asks if Louie is planning to go to college, Louie says, "Oh, not me, Coach. I ain't a brainiac." A little later in their conversation, Coach

Boone lowers his voice and says, "If you don't go to college, it's not going to be because you're not qualified, so I want you to bring me your test scores at the end of every week, and we'll go over them together, okay?"

Near the end of the movie, Louie tearfully approaches Coach Boone. "I got a C-plus average, Coach. I'm going to college." Because his coach took an interest in him Louie achieved more than he ever thought himself capable.

Most people are like that. They're looking for someone willing to invest in them, to encourage them to be the person God created them to be. Start looking for people who can use your encouragement and help.

## 4. ANYBODY WHO HELPS SOMEBODY INFLUENCES A LOT OF SOMEBODIES.

When you begin to pour your effort into helping someone else, it is absolutely amazing how that that encouragement gets multiplied. Influence influences. The greater the positive impact you make on another person, the more likely that person is to turn around and influence others positively. Encouragement has a ripple effect, like a stone dropped in a pool of water.

The problem is that we have a natural tendency to hold back. Why? Not because we don't want to meet the need, but because we're waiting for somebody else to do it. Encouragers can't think that way. They need to step out and start helping.

## 5. God Loves Everybody.

People tend to be too choosey about who they help and who they encourage. They look for people like themselves. And some people even believe that they should help only individuals who believe what they believe and think as they do. That's not the way it should be.

Years ago I came across a piece about someone who fell into a pit and couldn't get out—and how others treated that person:

> A subjective person came along and said, "I feel for you down there."
>
> An objective person came along and said, "Well, it's logical that someone would fall down there."
>
> A Pharisee said, "Only bad people fall into pits."
>
> A mathematician calculated how the individual fell into the pit.
>
> A news reporter wanted an exclusive story on the person in the pit.
>
> A fundamentalist said, "You deserve your pit."
>
> A Calvinist said, "If you'd been saved, you'd never fallen in that pit."

An Armenian said, "You were saved and still fell in that pit."

A charismatic said, "Just confess that you're not in that pit."

A realist came along and said: "Now that's a pit."

A geologist told him to appreciate the rock strata in the pit.

An IRS worker asked if he was paying taxes on this pit.

The county inspector asked if he had a permit to dig the pit.

A self-pitying person said, "You haven't seen anything until you've seen my pit."

An optimist said, "Things could be worse."

A pessimist said, "Things will get worse."

Jesus, seeing the man, reached down and took him by the hand and lifted him out of the pit.

We should always keep in mind that God loves everybody, and to treat others they way Jesus would treat them. Do that and others will always feel encouraged.

*Greet one another with a holy kiss.*

2 CORINTHIANS 13:12

# Reach Out to Those Close to You

A simple touch can convey an incredible
sense of love, affirmation, and acceptance.
A study conducted at UCLA several years
ago found that to maintain physical and
emotional health, men and women need
eight to ten meaningful touches each day.
These researchers defined meaningful touch
as a gentle tap, stroke, kiss, or hug, given by
a "significant other" such as a husband,
wife, parent, or close friend.

JAMES MERRITT,
*How to Be a Winner and Influence Anybody*

*Few things in the world*

*are more powerful*

*than a positive push.*

*A smile.*

*A word of optimism and hope.*

*A "you can do it"*

*when things are tough.*

RICHARD M. DEVOS

# A TEACHER'S WORDS CHANGE A LIFE

Antwone Fisher was born in an Ohio correctional facility while his mother was incarcerated. By then his father had already been dead for two months. As a result, he grew up a ward of the state in foster care. For longer than thirteen years, he lived with a couple who abused him horribly. Daily he was beaten down—physically, verbally, and psychologically. He never received a Christmas gift or a dime of allowance from his foster parents. For years he was the victim of sexual abuse. And he was often tied to a post in the basement and beaten. His foster mother used to brag that she had once beaten him until he was unconscious.

By the time Fisher entered the third grade, he had lost any natural love for learning. In addition, the constant admonition from his foster mother that he was the worst child in the world had convinced him that he couldn't learn and had no future. He failed fourth grade and was scheduled to repeat it. But then something wonderful happened. His foster family moved, which put him in a new school district. His new teacher was Mrs. Profit. "If there is such a thing as human beings who act as angels in our lives, Brenda Profit was that for me."[9]

Under Mrs. Profit's care, Fisher began to change his thinking about himself. He says, "If self-esteem was what you used to fill up like a tank of gas, the Picketts {his foster family} had siphoned mine out to nothing. Mrs. Profit helped changed all that."[40] Despite his gains, his academic progress was still meager by the end of the year. He was in danger of once again failing fourth grade. But then Fisher got another break. It was decided that Mrs. Profit would stay with her class of students and continue teaching them in fifth and sixth grades. Knowing that, she passed Fisher into the fifth grade. And it was then that an event occurred that would change his thinking forever.

It happened one day during reading. Fisher, a terribly shy child who sometimes stuttered, was asked to read aloud, and instead of panicking, he read well, including successfully sounding out a difficult word. Then Mrs. Profit praised him, saying, "I'm proud of you. I want you to know that I really struggled over promoting you, and I'm so glad that I did. You are doing very well this year." That's when something clicked in Fisher's head. He writes,

> Her honest, careful words are the equivalent of lightning bolts and thunderclaps. Outside I shyly accept her praise, but inside I'm flying with the birth of a revelation. It's the first time I've ever realized that there is something I can do to make things different for myself. Not just me, but anyone . . . . This lesson is a piece of gold I'll keep tucked in my back pocket for the rest of my life.[41]

In that moment, Fisher changed his thinking about himself—and it changed his life. He had plenty of ups and downs after that, but he knew he wasn't hopeless and a better future was possible for him. He didn't follow the path of his older foster brother and friends into a life of drugs and crime.

Today Antwone Fisher thinks for a living. He is a successful screenwriter in Hollywood. And he has become the kind of responsible citizen and family man he always desired to be, with a wife and daughter. When asked what message he wants his story to convey, his answer is, "That there is hope even when you have the hardest beginnings, and there are good people in the world."[12]

FROM *Today Matters*

*The best way*

*to cheer yourself up*

*is to cheer*

*everybody else up.*

MARK TWAIN

# BLESS AND BE BLESSED

Dan Clark recalls that when he was a teenager, he and his father once stood in line to buy tickets for the circus. As they waited, they noticed the family immediately in front of them. The parents were holding hands, and they had eight children in tow, all behaved well and all probably under the age of twelve. Based on their clean but simple clothing, he suspected they didn't have a lot of money. The kids jabbered about the exciting things they expected to see, and he could tell that the circus was going to be a new adventure for them.

As the couple approached the counter, the attendant asked how many tickets they wanted. The man proudly responded, "Please let me buy eight children's tickets and two adult tickets so I can take my family to the circus."

When the attendant quoted the price, the man's wife let go of his hand, and her head drooped. The man leaned a little closer and asked, "How much did you say?" The attendant again quoted the price. The man obviously didn't have enough money. He looked crushed.

Clark says his father watched all of this, put his hand in his pocket, pulled out a twenty-dollar bill, and dropped it on the ground. His father then reached down, picked up the bill, tapped the man on the shoulder, and said, "Excuse me, sir, this fell out of your pocket."

The man knew exactly what was going on. He looked straight into Clark's father's eyes, took his hand, shook it, and with a tear streaming down his cheek, replied, "Thank you, thank you, sir. This really means a lot to me and my family."

Clark and his father went back to their car and drove home. They didn't have enough money to go to the circus that night, but it didn't matter. They had encouraged a whole family. And it was something neither family would ever forget.

FROM *Winning with People*

No matter how busy you are,

you must take time

to make the other person important.

MARY KAY ASH

*Those who believe in our ability*

*do more than stimulate us.*

*They create for us an atmosphere*

*in which it becomes easier to succeed.*

JOHN H. SPALDING

# What You Need to Know to Encourage People

People are insecure . . . give them confidence.

People like to feel special . . . sincerely compliment them.

People are looking for a better tomorrow . . . show them hope.

People need to be understood . . . listen to them.

People lack direction . . . navigate for them.

People are selfish . . . speak to their needs first.

People get downhearted . . . encourage them.

People want to be associated with success . . . help them win.

People desire meaningful relationships . . . provide community.

People seek models to follow . . . be an example.

*Everyone has an invisible sign*

*hanging from his neck saying*

*Make Me Feel Important!*

*Never forget this message*

*when working with people.*

MARY KAY ASH

# HOW TO ADD VALUE TO OTHERS

People are always encouraged when another person invests in them, adding value to their lives. You can add value to others in the following ways:

WHEN YOU TRULY VALUE THEM. How do you show others that you value them? By believing in them before they believe in you. By serving them before they serve you. By loving them before they love you. By giving without expecting anything in return.

WHEN YOU MAKE YOURSELF MORE VALUABLE. You cannot give what you do not have. Good intentions never speak as loudly as good actions. Earn so that you can give. Grow so that you can mentor. Experience so that you can share wisdom.

WHEN YOU KNOW & RELATE TO WHAT THEY VALUE. What happens when you are focused entirely on your own agenda? You know little about the people around you. Stop and make others' priorities your priority. Ask to hear their stories. Find out about their hopes and dreams. Make their success part of your mission.

WHEN YOU DO THINGS THAT GOD VALUES. When your life is done, what will you have lived for? Everything on earth will eventually turn to dust—including you! Give yourself to things that will live on beyond your lifetime.

*Now may the God of patience and comfort grant you to be*

*like-minded toward one another, according to Christ Jesus,*

*that you may with one mind and one mouth glorify*

*the God and Father of our Lord Jesus Christ.*

ROMANS 15:5-6

# Encouragement

# Empowers Teams

The height of our love for God will never exceed

the depth of our love for one another.

PATRICK MORLEY

*The most important*

*single ingredient*

*in the formula*

*for success*

*is knowing how to*

*get along with people.*

THEODORE ROOSEVELT

# ENCOURAGE THE PLAYERS— BUILD THE TEAM

Have you ever been part of a losing team? It can be debilitating when spirits are low, the atmosphere is thick with infighting, and the team can't seem to get ahead.

What is the solution? Turn around the team's morale! Any time you can change the morale, you can change the team. Morale gives a team great power. Here's why I say that.

## 1. HIGH MORALE IS THE GREAT EXAGGERATOR.

When an entire team is positive and all the players feel good about themselves, *everything* seems good. Preparation seems to proceed more smoothly. Every break seems to go your way. The small victories seem sweet, and the big ones make you feel almost invincible. The stars of the team deliver at crunch time, and even the bench players seem to be playing beyond their usual capabilities.

Some people call such a time a winning streak or a stretch of good luck. But it's really just high morale. In sports, during times of high morale, everybody jumps onto the bandwagon as a fan. In big business, people buy the company's stock.

In entertainment, magazines and television networks ask for interviews—and producers pay top dollar for the team's services. Has the team changed from talentless to talented overnight? Is the team really as good as its press? Probably not. The team is enjoying the great exaggerator at work.

## 2. High Morale is the Great Elevator.

When a team possesses high morale, the performance of its people goes to a whole new level. The team focuses on its potential, not its problems. Team members become more committed. And everyone finds it easier to be unselfish. Team members are confident, and that confidence helps them to perform at a higher level.

When a team is losing, the opposite effect occurs. Players focus on their problems. Everyone's level of commitment goes down. The team repels others rather than attracts them. And everyone starts to look out for himself rather than his teammates. When you're losing, everything hurts.

## 3. High Morale is the Great Energizer.

High morale gives a team energy. Players become like the Energizer bunny: they keep going and going. No mountain seems too high. No project seems too difficult. No race seems too long. Their enthusiasm builds along with their energy, and the team develops a momentum that is almost unstoppable.

## 4. High Morale is the Great Eliminator.

Because of the momentum and energy that come with it, high morale also becomes the great eliminator. While a team that is losing and experiencing poor morale can be hurt by even the most minor problem, a team with high morale will keep right on going even when faced with a huge obstacle or otherwise disabling setback. Problems just seem to disappear—no matter how big they are.

## 5. High Morale is the Great Emancipator.

Something else that high morale does for a team is to free it up. Winning creates breathing room. A good team with high morale will use that breathing room to take risks and try out new ideas, new moves, new concepts that it otherwise wouldn't. It stops to ask questions that it otherwise might not. And doing these things yields creativity and innovation. In the end, high morale releases the team to reach its potential

So if you're on a team with low morale, how do you turn things around? How do you get the positive momentum started? You start with encouragement. People who feel encouraged work a little bit harder. They feel a little bit better about themselves. They feel a little more positive about their teammates. They start to believe they can win. Any little bit of success breeds more success—especially if team leaders and team members continue to encourage one another when they stumble or fall.

If you want to turn a team around, help to turn each individual player around. Won't you also need to improve the way you do things? Probably. Won't you have to eliminate some players and find better ones to take their place? Possibly. But you'll never know what you've got until you encourage who you've got. Help each person to make the most of his or her talent, and there's no telling how far the team can go.

ADAPTED FROM

*The 17 Indisputable Laws of Teamwork*

I'm just a plowhand from Arkansas, but I have learned how to hold a team together. How to lift some men up, how to calm down others, until finally they've got one heartbeat together, a team. There's just three things I'd ever say:

*If anything goes bad, I did it.*
*If anything goes semi-good, then we did it.*
*If anything goes real good, then you did it.*

That's all it takes to get people to win football games for you.

BEAR BRYANT

# TWO DIFFERENT KINDS
# OF LEADERS

During the second half of the nineteenth century, two strong men vied for leadership of Great Britain's government: William Gladstone and Benjamin Disraeli. These two politicians were intense rivals. You can detect how they felt about one another based on a comment once made by Disraeli: "The difference between a misfortune and a calamity? If Gladstone fell into the Thames ⸢River⸣, it would be a misfortune. But if someone dragged him out again, it would be a calamity."

Gladstone, leader of the Liberal party for three decades, is considered by many to personify the best qualities of Victorian England. A career public servant, he was a great orator, a master of finance, and a staunchly moral man. He was made Prime Minister of the United Kingdom four different times, the only person in the nation's history to achieve that honor. Under his leadership, Great Britain established a national education system, instituted parliamentary reform, and saw the vote given to a significant number of people in the working classes.

Benjamin Disraeli, who himself served twice as Prime Minister, had a different kind of background. In his thirties, he entered politics and built a reputation as a diplomat and social reformer. But his greatest accomplishment was masterminding Great Britain's purchase of shares in the Suez Canal.

Although both men accomplished much for Britain, what really separated them as leaders was their approach to people. The difference can be best illustrated by a story told by a young woman who dined with the two rival statesmen on consecutive nights. When asked her impression of them, she said, "When I left the dining room after sitting next to Mr. Gladstone, I thought he was the cleverest man in England. But after sitting next to Mr. Disraeli, I thought I was the cleverest woman in England."

There's a lesson here about leadership. Leaders can win the confidence, trust, and friendship of the people they lead by taking the spotlight off of themselves and putting it on others. In fact, this principle works in all areas of life.

ADAPTED FROM
*The 21 Indispensable Qualities of a Leader*

*Let nothing be done*

*through selfish ambition or conceit,*

*but in lowliness of mind let each*

*esteem others better than himself.*

*Let each of you look out*

*not only for his own interests,*

*but also to the interests of others.*

PHILIPPIANS 2:3-4

# Honor the Whole Team

People who build successful teams never forget that every person's role is contributing to the bigger picture.

One of the best examples of this involves Winston Churchill. During the darkest days of World War II, Great Britain had a difficult time keeping men working in the coal mines. Many wanted to give up their dirty, thankless jobs in the dangerous mines to join the military service, which got much public praise and support. Yet without coal, the military and the people at home would be in trouble.

So Churchill faced thousands of coal miners one day and passionately told them of their importance to the war effort, how their role could make or break the goal of maintaining England's freedom. It's said that tears appeared in the eyes of those hardened men. And they returned to their inglorious work with steely resolve.

Everyone needs encouragement. Just letting someone know their work is appreciated makes a team run more smoothly, becoming stronger and more effective.

*The nice thing about*

*teamwork is that*

*you always have*

*others on your side.*

Margaret Carty

# TO IMPROVE YOUR TEAM, LIFT UP YOUR TEAMMATES

Team members always love and admire a player who is able to help them go to another level, someone who enlarges them and empowers them to be successful. Those kinds of people are like the Boston Celtics' hall-of-fame center Bill Russell, who said, "The most important measure of how good a game I played was how much better I'd made my teammates play."

Players who enlarge their teammates have several things in common:

## 1. ENLARGERS VALUE THEIR TEAMMATES.

Industrialist Charles Schwab observed, "I have yet to find the man, however exalted his station, who did not do better work and put forth greater effort under a spirit of approval than under a spirit of criticism." Your teammates can tell whether you believe in them. People's performances usually reflect the expectations of those they respect.

## 2. ENLARGERS KNOW AND RELATE TO WHAT THEIR TEAMMATES VALUE

Players who enlarge others listen to discover what their teammates talk about, and they watch to see what teammates spend their money on. That kind of knowledge, along with a desire to relate to their fellow players, creates a strong connection between people. And it makes possible an enlarger's next characteristic.

## 3. ENLARGERS ADD VALUE TO THEIR TEAMMATES.

Adding value is really the essence of enlarging others. It's finding ways to help others improve their abilities and attitudes. An enlarger looks for the gifts, talents, and uniqueness in other people, and then helps them to increase those abilities for their benefit and for that of the entire team. An enlarger is able to take others to a whole new level.

## 4. ENLARGERS MAKE THEMSELVES MORE VALUABLE

Enlargers work to make themselves better, not only because it benefits them personally, but because it helps them to help others. You cannot give what you do not have. For example, in basketball a great player like Karl Malone was often aided by a great passer like all-time assist leader John Stockton. In football, a great receiver like Jerry Rice was made better by great quarterbacks, such as Joe Montana and Steve Young. If you want to increase the ability of a teammate, make yourself better.

FROM *The 17 Essential Qualities*
*of a Team Player*

*Eye has not seen, nor ear heard,*

*Nor have entered into the heart of man*

*The things which God has prepared for those who love Him.*

1 CORINTHIANS 2:9

# Encouragement

# Leads to Great Things

*An automobile goes nowhere efficiently unless it has a quick,*

*hot spark to ignite things, to set the cogs of the machine in motion.*

*So I try to make every player on my team feel he's the spark*

*keeping our machine in motion.*

KNUTE ROCKNE

*Trust men and they will be true to you;*

*treat them greatly and they will show themselves great.*

RALPH WALDO EMERSON

# BEHIND EVERY GREAT PERSON
## IS A GREAT ENCOURAGER

Everybody needs somebody. None of us achieves anything without help from someone else. Some of the greatest achievers in history became all that they did because of the people in their lives.

In recent years, moviegoers have enjoyed film versions of *The Chronicles of Narnia* and *The Lord of the Rings*. Most people are aware that the movies were based on books. What many don't know is that their authors, C. S. Lewis and J. R. R. Tolkien, were professors at Oxford University and maintained a close friendship throughout their careers. Every Thursday they, along with other writers, would meet together to have a drink, talk about their fiction-writing endeavors, and read passages of their yet unpublished works.

It was Tolkien who challenged and encouraged Lewis, an avowed atheist, to explore Christianity, ultimating leading to his conversion. And it was Lewis who encouraged Tolkien to continue writing fiction and to seek publication. Were it not for their friendship and mutual encouragement, the world would not have received the finest writing in apologetics of the twentieth century nor perhaps the finest fantasy work ever written.

Though their case may seem unusual, if you look at the achievements of great people, you often find that they were encouraged by a likeminded or admiring friend.

AUTOMOBILE GIANT HENRY FORD and the prolific inventor Thomas Edison were friends and neighbors for years. They first met at a convention sponsored by Edison's company, where Ford worked as an engineer. Someone pointed out Ford to Edison as "a young man who has made a gas car." Ford and Edison talked a while about the automobile, and Edison suddenly banged a fist down on the table with excitement. "You have it! Your car is self-contained and carries its own power plant."

Ford later remembered of their first meeting: "No man up to then had given me any encouragement. I had hoped that I was headed right. Sometimes I knew that I was, sometimes I only wondered, but here, all at once and out of a clear sky, the greatest inventive genius in the world had given me complete approval."[13] The two men worked, traveled, and enjoyed time together for years to come.

HYMNIST CHARLES WESLEY was suffering a severe bout with pleurisy and was plagued by doubts about his faith when a group of Christians visited him. They took care of him and told stories about God's work in their lives. After their visit, Wesley felt strengthened not only in body but also in soul. He wrote the popular hymn "O for a Thousand Tongues to Sing" as a result and went on to write many, many others, making a large contribution to the catalogue of church music.

Sir Isaac Newton, considered by many to be the most influential scientist of the modern era, is best known for his theory of gravitation and description of the three laws of motion. But Newton might never have published his work in that area had it not been for Edmond Halley. A well respected scientist in his own right, Halley visited Newton at Cambridge to discuss a problem he was working on only to discover that Newton had already solved it. Halley encouraged Newton to publish his work. And Halley even offered to do it at his own expense. The result was the publication of *Principia Mathematica Philosophiae Naturalis* in 1687, which laid the groundwork for the study of mechanics and changed the way people see the world.

Esther, the young Jewish woman after whom the book in the Bible is named, became a queen when she married King Xerxes of Persia. When the king's chief advisor plotted the Jews' destruction, Esther's uncle Mordecai encouraged her to step out in faith and intercede on behalf of her people, telling her, "who knows whether you have come to the kingdom for such a time as this?" (Esther 4:14). When she found the courage to approach the king, she saved her people.

Look at the lives of people who accomplish great things, and you find encouragers who helped them along the way.

Who can you encourage to do great things? Who has God put into your life to cheer on, raise up, and assist on their journey? Help others to do the things God created them to do, and you share in their achievement.

In Catherine Ryan Hyde's novel *Pay It Forward* and the subsequent movie, twelve-year-old Trevor McKinney comes up with a simple—but incredibly profound—plan to change the world: He will do something good for three people and ask them to, rather than paying him back, to pay it forward by doing something to help three more people. The result, he reasons, will be a wave of changed lives throughout the world. In the end, this one twelve-year-old boy makes life better for his mother, his teacher, and countless people he'd never even met.

Even the smallest acts of kindness and encouragement can multiply in the lives of others, snowballing into something bigger than we ever could have imagined.

*Every beginning is a consequence.*

*Every beginning ends something.*

PAUL VALÉRY

*Most of the things*
*worth doing in the world*
*had been declared impossible*
*before they were done.*

AUTHOR UNKNOWN

# Don't Expect Encouragement from "Experts"

In the course of every day, you will encounter small-minded, negative individuals. Don't let them squelch your enthusiasm or cloud your vision. Never let them steal your dreams. What they present as wisdom, is sometimes merely short-sightedness. Consider these statements from so-called experts:

*"Heavier-than-air flying machines are not possible."*
LORD KELVIN, *president of England's Royal Society, 1895*

*"Everything that can be invented has been invented."*
CHARLES H. DUELL, *director of the U.S. Patent Office, 1899*

*"Sensible and responsible women do not want to vote."*
GROVER CLEVELAND, *U.S. President, 1905*

*"There is no likelihood man can ever tap the power of the atom."*
ROBERT MILLIKEN, *Nobel Prize winner in Physics, 1923*

Never forget: We go where our dreams take us.

# THE POWER OF PASSION

"Experts" spend a lot of time trying to figure out what makes people successful, and more than anything else, passion is what makes the difference. Take a look at four truths about passion:

PASSION IS THE FIRST STEP TO ACHIEVEMENT. Your desire determines your destiny. The stronger your fire, the greater the desire—and the greater the potential.

PASSION INCREASES YOUR WILLPOWER. There is no substitute for passion. It is the fuel for the will. If you want anything badly enough, you can find the willpower to achieve it.

PASSION CHANGES YOU. If you follow your passion you can't help but become a more dedicated, productive person. In the end, your passion will have more influence than your personality.

PASSION MAKES THE IMPOSSIBLE POSSIBLE. Humans are made so that whenever anything fires their soul, impossibilities vanish. A fire in the heart lifts everything in life.

When we find our passion, we can be assured that great things do lie ahead. What can you do to find yours—and what can you do to help someone else find theirs?

*Your friends will*

*encourage your vision*

*or choke your dream.*

AUTHOR UNKNOWN

*As important as your past is,*

*it's not as important as the way*

*you see your future.*

JOHN C. MAXWELL

# HIS EARLY PASSION KEEPS HIM ENCOURAGING

What does a boy like Rueben Martinez do in a place like Miami, Arizona? Miami is a small mining town of two thousand people in the southeastern part of Arizona that had changed little since its founding in 1907. When Martinez was growing up in the 1940s and 1950s, most of the town's jobs came from the copper mining industry, as they still do. His parents, who were Mexican immigrants, worked in the mines. There wasn't much to do in Miami. But Martinez had a curious mind, and he found his passion in books—not necessarily an easy task when your parents aren't big readers and your town is so small that it doesn't even have a public library.

"My mother always wanted me to put down my books and clean the yard," recalls Martinez. "So I would hide in the outhouse and read because no one would bother me there."[14]

The child was so desperate for reading material that he became very industrious. "Every morning at 6:45," he says, "the newspaper boy would deliver the newspaper and, when it hit my neighbor's side of the house, I would wake up, go out the back door, lean against my neighbor's house, and read the newspaper every morning thoroughly. Then I'd fold that newspaper and put it back as neatly as I could."[45]

Eventually Martinez got caught. But his neighbor didn't mind and encouraged him to keep reading. Martinez was also inspired and assisted by two of his teachers. They continually encouraged his love of reading and loaned him books.

Martinez moved to California and went on to become a barber. But the passion for reading that was encouraged as a boy continued to grow. When he owned his own barber shop, he began lending out volumes from his two-hundred-book collection. But when they often went unreturned, he came up with another solution. He started selling books. A few years later, the barbershop with books became a bookstore with a symbolic barber chair. Martinez called his store Librería Martínez Books and Art Gallery.

"We started out with two books," says Martinez, "then ten, then twenty-five. Little by little, we've sold over two million books. That's what happens if you dare to dream."[46] The store now stocks seventeen thousand titles and has become one of the country's largest suppliers of Spanish-language books. Martinez opened a second store in 2004 and also a third store just for children.

He tells parents, "Do you want your child to be ahead of the line or at the back of the line, moms and dads? You have to support, endorse, and read to your kid . . . if you do that, your kid will be at the head of the line . . . and be someone special in this world. Reading does it."

People are starting to recognize Martinez's talent. In 2004, he won a MacArthur Foundation fellowship—often called a "genius grant"—for "fusing the roles of marketplace and community center to inspire appreciation of literature and preserve Latino literary heritage." He became the U.S. Small Business Administration's 2004 Minority Business Advocate of the Year. He received an honorary doctorate in humane letters from Whittier College in 2005 and was also named one of Inc.com's twenty-six most fascinating entrepreneurs.

Martinez isn't stopping. In his mid-sixties, he has no intention of resting on his laurels. He is energized by what he does.

"I made more money cutting hair than selling books," notes Martinez. "But the joy of my life is what I'm doing now." Martinez wants to create a bilingual Borders-style chain of bookstores across the nation, hoping to establish twenty-five stores by 2012. He has probably encouraged more Hispanic readers in the United States than any other individual.

"If I had stayed with my factory jobs," observes Martinez, "I would have been living a comfortable retirement now. But I chose to go on my own as a barber. Now with the bookstores, I'm going to work for the rest of my life."

Adapted from *Talent is Never Enough*

*You have never*

*tested God's resources*

*until you have*

*attempted the impossible.*

AUTHOR UNKNOWN

# EPILOGUE
### *Bless and Be Blessed*

Business professors Gary Hamel and C. K. Prahalad have written about an experiment that was conducted with a group of monkeys. Four monkeys were placed in a room that had a tall pole in the center of it. Suspended from the top of that pole was a bunch of bananas. One of the hungry monkeys started climbing the pole to get something to eat, but just as it reached out to grab a banana, it was doused with a torrent of cold water. Squealing, he scampered down the pole and abandoned its attempt to feed himself. Each monkey made a similar attempt, and each one was drenched with cold water. After making several attempts, they finally gave up.

Then researchers removed one of the monkeys from the room and replaced it with a new monkey. As the newcomer began to climb the pole, the other three grabbed it and pulled it down to the ground. After trying to climb the pole several times and being dragged down by the others, it finally gave up and never attempted to climb the pole again.

One by one, the researchers replaced the original monkeys with new ones, and each time a new monkey was brought in, It would be dragged down by the others before it could reach the bananas. In time, the room was filled with monkeys that had never received a cold shower. None of them would climb the pole, but not one of them knew why.

Sometimes, we can feel like those monkeys. We live in a world where many people seem to hold us down when we want to climb and reach for our dreams. Sadly, they often do it because they are trying to be helpful.

The antidote is encouragement. Encouragement changes everything! By encouraging others and creating an atmosphere of encouragement for the people around us, we have the power to improve the lives of others.

As you seek to encourage others, be encouraged by these heartening promises from Scripture:

> *You hear, O LORD , the desire of the afflicted;*
> *you encourage them, and you listen to their cry*
> *(Psalm 10:17 NIV).*

> *Do not be afraid. Stand still, and see the salvation*
> *of the LORD , which He will accomplish for you today*
> *(Exodus 14:13).*

*{The LORD } is the One who goes before you.*
*He will be with you, He will not leave you nor forsake you;*
*do not fear nor be dismayed (Deuteronomy 31:8).*

*May the LORD bring good to you and keep you.*
*May the LORD make His face shine upon you, and be kind to you.*
*May the LORD show favor toward you, and give you peace*
*(Numbers 6:24–26 NLT).*

Encouragement really does change everything. May you be blessed by God, and share that blessing in encouragement to the people in your life!

*A bold heart is half the battle.*

DWIGHT D. EISENHOWER

# NOTES

1 "Father-Son Duo Are World Class Competitors, Despite Odds," CNN.com, 29 November 1999.

2 Ibid.

3 Ibid.

4 Ibid.

5 Mohney, Nell. "Beliefs Can Influence Attitudes." *Kingsport Times-News.* July 25, 1986. P 4B.

6 George W. Crane, *Dr. Crane's Radio Talks*, vol. 1 (Mellot, IN: Hopkis Syndicate, Inc., 1948), 7.

7 Ibid., 8-9.

8 Ibid., 16.

9 Antwone Quenton Fisher with Mim Eichler Rivas, *Finding Fish* (New York: Perennial, 2001), 122.

10 Ibid, 125.

11 Ibid, 127.

12 Rebecca Murray, "The Real Antwone Fisher Talks About the Movie, 'Antwone Fisher,'" http://romanticmovies.about.com/library/weekly/aaantwonefisherintc.htm, 25 July 2003.

13 Patricia Zacharias, "Henry Ford and Thomas Edison—a friendship of giants." The Detroit News. http://info.detnews.com/history/story/index.cfm?id=105&category=people Accessed 14 July 2007.

14 Ana Figueroa, "Rueben Martinez: Barber and Book Lover," *AARP Segunda Juventud,* April/May 2005, http://www.aarpsegundajuventud.org/english/nosotros/2005-AM/05AM_bookshop.html.

15 "Life and Times" (transcript), KCET News, 11 November 2004, http://www.kcet.org/lifeandtimes/archives/200411109.php

16 Figueroa, "Rueben Martinez: Barber and Book Lover."

# JOHN C. MAXWELL

is an internationally recognized leadership expert, speaker, and author who has sold over 13 million books. His organizations have trained more than 2 million leaders worldwide. Dr. Maxwell is the founder of EQUIP and INJOY Stewardship Services. Every year he speaks to Fortune 500 companies, international government leaders, and organizations as diverse as the United States Military Academy at West Point and the National Football League. A *New York Times*, *Wall Street Journal*, and *Business Week* best-selling author, Maxwell was named the World's Top Leadership Guru by Leadershipgurus.net. He was also one of only 25 authors and artists named to Amazon.com's 10th Anniversary Hall of Fame. Three of his books, *The 21 Irrefutable Laws of Leadership*, *Developing the Leader Within You*, and *The 21 Indispensable Qualities of a Leader*, have each sold over a million copies.